DR. LESTER SUMRALL

THE MYSTERY OF IMMORTALITY

Avoiding
the Pain and
Consequences of
Moral Sin!

Unless otherwise indicated,
all Scripture quotations are taken from
the *King James Version* of the Bible.

The Mystery of Immortality
ISBN 0-937580-09-0
Copyright © 1989 by
Lester Sumrall Evangelistic Association
Published by LESEA Publishing Company
P.O. Box 12
South Bend, Indiana 46624

CONTENTS

INTRODUCTION

Immortality is one of the hottest debated subjects of our time. The most controversial of all topics in the universe.

Buddhists teach transmigration of the soul through reincarnation. Hindus teach that man in his next life can take on animal life or even become an insect. Catholics teach about an intermediary place—purgatory—where purging for sins and payment of money is man's destiny.

What is the truth about the eternalness of man?

The Communists teach that man is not immortal.

The infidels teach that man is not immortal.

The rationalists teach that man is not immortal.

The evolutionists teach that man is not immortal.

The humanists teach that man is not immortal.

They are wandering in mental darkness and in the abyss of demon inspired lies.

Come let us get acquainted with life and immortality. In the final analysis nothing is so exciting as a probe into the mystery of immortality.

1

HOW HUMAN IMMORTALITY CAME TO BE

And the LORD God formed man of the dust of the ground, and breathed into his nostrils the breath of life; and man became a living soul.
Genesis 2:7

GOD has power, but God is love. It is possible that no human intelligence will ever comprehend the magnitude of the true essence of Jehovah-God, until we are living with Him in eternity!

The essential nature of love demands an object to be loved. Love cannot be contained in a static condition. It demands expression. It demands life. Love without expression is dead.

Now, "God is love" (1 John 4:16). This is the true revelation of the divine purposes which motivated God to create the universe. It was the magnificence of His personality expressing itself in creative grandeur. With His fingers of omnipotence and omniscience, He arranged the mighty constellations in space. The stars, planets and suns are innumerable. I, personally, heard an astronomer at the observatory in Chicago say that science is convinced that there are as many stars in the universe as there are grains of sand upon the seashores of the world! When God created this resplendent array of indescribable glory, He walked down the "Milky Way" and, though its dazzling brilliance stood before Him in cosmic beauty, He felt it lacked something. *It could not return His love.*

Therefore, the heart of God was not satisfied. God then turned to one of the smallest of these planets—the earth—and, with the Word of His mouth, spoke mountains into upraised strength and glory. He crested their towering peaks in white, making them beautiful to look upon. He spread out the boundless seas in the palm of His hand and listened to their glorious roaring. He planted the valleys with a luxuriant growth of palms and flowers. He populated the forests with the strong denizens of the deep wood. As God beheld the handiwork of His genius, it was beautiful to look upon. It was intriguing to observe, but there was nothing that could truly and intelligently return His love.

Love must be reciprocal. Love must be intelligent. The heart of God yearned for a return of love.

Standing in the midst of this radiant, creative glory, God stooped down and took some red earth and, maybe shedding a tear to moisten it, molded a creature in His own image. There it lay, inanimate, the very semblance of Himself. God was pleased with this work and He breathed upon it and His own vibrating life force ran into every part of that creature. Adam opened his eyes and God saw something in those eyes that made Him know He would be satisfied. Adam smiled, and God knew this creature could return His love. Adam stood upright and God went for a walk with him through the garden he had prepared for this creature who was made in His own image! He could now love this new creation and this creature could love Him. The words of Jesus spoken millenia later became vibrantly true, "God so loved the world. . ." (John 3:16).

Adam was a part of the new world! He walked with God. He talked with God.

As God observed this new creation He said, "I can give it one gift more. I can have it join me in reproductive power. I can permit it to work with me in procreation. I can have this beautiful creation, Adam, make others like himself and then not only will he love me but he will love others like himself!"

Thus God saw, in His perfect wisdom, that He must create a woman (a womb-man). Rather than beginning again in the dust, He became the world's first surgeon. He took from inside the body of Adam, a portion of his body and from that created a perfect woman and sat her beside Adam.

God now had two objects to love Him, and they loved one another. This gave God the possibilities of unlimited love as He bade man and woman become one flesh in "replenishing the earth."

THE MYSTERY OF LIFE

God performed the first wedding ceremony and united Adam and Eve. He gave them a secret, "You can now produce immortal souls who will never die. This is the highest honor that I can bestow upon you. This is the most sacred function of your existence. This must be guarded with the keys of your heart and in this matter you must never fail me. If you build a house, it will fall. If you build a nation or an empire, it will die, but these immortal creatures which you shall produce can never die!"

In this way God permitted man to

join Him in divinity and in the mystery of life. Life is the greatest mystery in our world. There are many mysteries surrounding mankind, but the greatest is how two protoplasmic cells unite and generate life.

God is the giver of all life.

The Lord Jesus Christ said, "I am the way, the truth and the life," (John 14:6). He is Life because He is God!

This book is written around the true meaning of immortality and the sacredness of "reproducing after its kind."

God speaks to our generation in Proverbs 6:32-33:

"But whoso committeth adultery with a woman lacketh understanding: He that doeth it destroyeth his own soul.

"A wound and dishonour shall he get; And his reproach shall not be wiped away."

God means that if you trifle with the elements of immortality it is like putting your fingers on a hot stove; you get burned.

Now let's proceed.

2

THE MYSTERY OF
IMMORTALITY

*For none of us lives to himself,
and no one dies to himself. For if we live,
we live to the Lord; and if we die,
we die to the Lord. Therefore, whether we
live or die, we are the Lord's.*
Romans 14:7-8 NKJ

IMMORTALITY is man's greatest mystery. Every Homo sapien born on planet earth is indelibly stamped with immortality. He or she will live forever either in the sublime light of heaven, or the infernal darkness of hell.

How to understand and determine the value of this eternalness is man's greatest achievement.

How can we understand immortality?

Immortality is revealed to man by a knowledge of Christ. John 1:4 says, "In him was life; and the life was the light of men." And in John 5:24, "He that heareth my word, and believeth on him that sent me, hath everlasting life, and shall not pass into condemnation; but is passed from death unto life." Therefore all understanding of eternal life is through Christ.

In 1 John 5:11 we are told, "And this is the record, that God hath given to us eternal life, and this life is in his Son."

Some people call you a bigot if you start quoting the Bible. They say, "There are other ways to heaven than Jesus and all the different religions are all going to the same place."

But if you go one direction on a superhighway and others go the other way, you won't arrive at the same destination.

The mystery of immortality is revealed to us by Jesus Christ in John 5:40, "And ye will not come to me, that ye might have life."

Also, Jesus said in Matthew 25:46, "And these shall go away unto everlasting punishment: but the righteous into life eternal."

This verse reveals the partings of the immortals. At a certain time in history God says one person goes into eternal darkness, and another goes into eternal life.

Immortality is revealed by reigning with Christ, "For if by one man's offence death reigned by one; much more they which receive abundance of grace and of the gift of righteousness shall reign in life by one Jesus Christ" (Romans 5:17).

"Marvel not at this: for the hour is coming, in the which all that are in the graves shall hear his voice,

"And shall come forth; they that have done good, unto the resurrection of life; and they that have done evil, unto the resurrection of damnation" (John 5:28-29).

The Apostle Paul said in Galatians 6:8, ". . .He that soweth to his flesh shall of the flesh reap corruption; but he that soweth to the Spirit shall of the Spirit reap life everlasting."

The Apostle John said in Revelation 3:5, "He that overcometh, the same shall be clothed in white (raiment); and I will not blot out his name out of the book of life, but I will confess his name before my Father, and before his angels."

In 1 Corinthians 15:51-57 the Holy Spirit says, "Behold, I show you a mystery; We shall not all sleep, but we shall all be changed, in a moment, in the twinkling of an eye, at the last trump: for the trumpet shall sound, and the dead shall be raised incorruptible, and we shall be changed.

"For this corruptible must put on incorruption, and this mortal must put on immortality.

"So when this corruptible shall have put on incorruption, and this mortal shall have put on immortality, then shall be brought to pass the saying that is written, Death is swallowed up in victory.

"O death, where is thy sting? O grave, where is thy victory?

"The sting of death is sin; and the strength of sin is the law.

"But thanks be to God, which giveth us the victory through our Lord Jesus Christ."

Man finally arrives at his eternal habitation.

3

WHY IS ADULTERY INVOLVED IN IMMORTALITY?

Thou shalt not commit adultery.
Exodus 20:14

THE Bible speaks strongly against adultery.

The first reference to adultery is found in the Ten Commandments (Exodus 20:14). In fact, there was a time when the adulterer and adulteress were put to death when discovered.

"And the man that committeth adultery with another man's wife, . . .the adulterer and the adulteress shall surely be put to death" (Leviticus 20:10).

God has never winked at immortality. Is there one sin or transgression which carries more hurt than other sins?

Does society have an unforgivable sin—a sin it refuses to forget—a scarlet sin?

When we study the pages of history we discover that men or women who refuse to live correct morally, very often find themselves in an unforgivable position among men. Even though people say they forgive, they seldom forget this sin! It is a blot that cannot easily be erased. It is a scar that refuses to heal.

Solomon said: "But whoso committeth adultery with a woman lacketh understanding: he that doeth it destroyeth his own soul. A wound and dishonour shall he get; and his reproach shall not be wiped away" (Proverbs 6:32-33).

PRINCIPLE OF LIFE

Why is this fact so inherent in the human race?

Why is it more forcibly followed among primitive people than more culturally advanced folk? Why is history so seemingly cruel in indelibly marking those who sin morally?

I was kneeling in prayer in Hong Kong when God revealed to me that this was true because this sin was a transgression against His principle of life. He showed me that when He gave the commandment in Exodus 20:14, "Thou shalt not commit adultery," it was not to deny man any joy or pleasure which should be his as an intelligent creature. It was a deeper and more meaningful aspect of life; adultery or any immoral perversion touches the fountain of life and corrupts it.

God, in His determinate will, chose to make man a procreator with Himself. God could have made men the same as He did angels—neither male nor female—but He didn't. God chose, in His sovereign might, to permit you and me to reproduce other men and women; to be procreators with Him.

By the union of Adam and Eve, it became possible to produce a unity of one—a new one. God created Adam and God made Eve, but Adam and Eve produced Abel, Cain and Seth.

God chose to let man become almost as God, a creator who could bring into being one who looks like himself—one he can hold in his arms and say, "Look at this baby. He resembles me!"

This is the greatest possession in the world; greater than getting a new automobile or a new house. There is one thing truly precious, that is to bring into this world an immortal creature—a soul who will live forever!

When a person produces life, he is acting in the capacity of a creator and is very closely associated with divinity. Therefore, when a man or woman illegitimately touches that source of life, God finds it difficult to forgive him and his fellow man finds it nearly impossible to forgive. Society will not forgive that sin. They'll talk about it (and you) behind your back for the rest of your life.

Because of this sin in the world, there are millions of people who are deformed and insane, who possess strange lusts that no psychiatrist can understand. This transgression unless confessed to God and abandoned, finally brings the soul of man to an eternal hell because he tampered with the source and the mystery of immortality, unless the man or woman confesses. Repentance and conversion restores a man or woman.

God showed me that other sins, although they will take you to hell, are not like this sin. Life is sacred with God and everything that pertains to the creation of life is sacred to Him. Man has been set in a place higher than angels (Hebrews 1:4). Angels cannot produce children; they cannot produce angels. This privilege is so sacred to God that the person who violates this great principle of immortality becomes a marked person.

Ask yourself this: If you were writing my life story, wouldn't you write all the good things you knew about me, rather than the bad? From biographies of George Washington, you might think he was an angel, but of course he was not an angel. There were a lot of very negative things about his life. When men write the uncritical life story of a great man, they write only that he was a good and great man, but, when God writes a man's story, He puts everything down—the bad along with the good!

For example, God loved David but, when David sinned, He still put it in His book, the Bible. God loved Samson, too, but when Samson sinned God also put that account in His book—because God hates sin. God especially hates anything that tampers with the source of life which began in the Garden of Eden.

God placed man in the amazing position of being a partaker of God's deity. Man possesses the power, with God, to produce a soul that will never die! What a tremendous responsibility this is! An oak tree produces acorns which produce other oak trees which will eventually die and disintegrate, but man produces immortal souls that will live throughout the endless ages of eternity!

When this great truth dawned upon

me in Hong Kong, I jumped up and walked back and forth praying: "Oh God, Oh God, help me to show people they must not commit adultery, because it is tampering with a life source of the universe!"

Talk about atomic bombs and nuclear power. This is something more explosive! This is earth's greatest power! It is the mind which explores all other energy.

THOSE WHO COMMIT
IMMORAL SINS

When any thoughtful person leafs back through the pages of human history he poignantly discovers that men, women, and nations who refused to live correct moral lives placed themselves in an unfavorable and often an unforgivable position. This can be proven beyond discussion.

DAVID AND BATHSHEBA

One of the most remembered biblical examples is King David. The Bible declares that David was a man after God's own heart. Anyone who reads the book of Psalms, the largest book in the Bible, knows that no other person ever sought after God more than David. Yet, David sinned morally and it marred his life.

Millions of people, through the ages, have forgotten that King David was one of the bravest warriors who ever lived. When you read of his daring exploits you see a true superman, for David was born with a brave heart.

When he was a mere boy, a radiant youth, he went to battle against a towering bully who was about ten feet tall and had six fingers on each hand and six toes on each foot. This ungodly Philistine, named Goliath, had struck fear into the entire army of Israel. In the whole nation not one brave man stepped forward to accept his challenge to a dual.

It was this daring David, who, without sword or spear, walked into an open battle arena, with only a slingshot in his hand. While boastful Goliath was screaming insults at him, he wound up that slingshot and made an impression in that giant's head that the world reads about 3,000 years later!

This mocking, ridiculing enemy of Israel fell headlong to the ground. David ran forward and used the giant's own sword to destroy him.

It took real courage to be such a man as David. He not only killed giants but, with his bare hands, went into mortal battle with a bear and then with a lion. David, not satisfied with such plaudits, displayed one of the greatest combinations of talents known in history when he became a national administrator, a great judge and a famous king. David molded twelve disorganized tribes of people into a first class nation called Israel. David was a real leader and statesman.

In spite of all this, few people today think of David in that capacity. Our world does not sing the sweet songs of David. They forget how he played upon his harp and sang before a mad king—a king depressed to the point of insanity—songs that could quiet his troubled soul and spirit. King Saul was so belligerent he, at times, even attempted to kill his entertainer, but David's singing and playing were so skillful and anointed that they transformed the heart of King Saul from sadness to gladness! Talk about tranquilizers, David was a living tranquilizer!

In spite of all this, who today remembers these things about David? What the world remembers is that he committed adultery with Bathsheba. You may ask almost any sinner on the street, "What do you know about King David?" He will sarcastically reply, "Why, he is the guy who stole another man's wife!"

One day, while sitting in a barber shop waiting to get a haircut, I spoke to a man sitting next to me and asked him to accept Christ as his Savior. Before he could answer, another man in the shop spoke up and said, "Now, about that religion you have, explain to me why David committed adultery and had his neighbor killed; yet the Bible says that he was a man after God's own heart. What kind of heart does God have?"

I tried to explain to everyone's satisfaction that David was backslidden and out of touch with God at that time. Still David's sin, committed 3,000 years ago, kept me from convincing that man and winning that soul!

Can you now see how adultery becomes a sin related to immortality? Here were sinners, 3,000 years later, mocking David. If David had not sinned, just consider what the modern world would think of him today. If they had only the stories of his daring bravery, his sweet songs and of his outstanding statesmanship, instead, because of this recorded instance of uncontrolled passion, people mock him to this day. Even gaudy, sinful Hollywood makes pictures about David and Bathsheba. Even there, he is a laughingstock to the world. The world has not forgotten. Public opinion has not forgiven him. For other sins or blunders history would have pardoned him, but not for this sin against immortality!

SAMSON AND DELILAH

Another striking example of this truth is the Bible story of the great man Samson. Of all humans who have ever lived, he is recorded as the strongest. Samson possessed strength that no other human, before or since, has ever equaled. The Bible declares that, on one occasion, Samson caught three hundred foxes single-handed! Of course, this is a miracle. On another occasion, a lion attacked Samson. This young man, with the strength of his Nazarite vow flowing through him, took that young lion by the top of his mouth and lower part of his mouth and, with the superhuman strength that God had given him, pulled until the jaw sockets came loose and the lion fell over dead.

On another occasion, Samson went out to fight the enemies of Israel and, not having a conventional weapon, he picked up the jawbone of a dead ass and, with this jawbone Samson began to strike the warriors of Philistia and slew a thousand men. After the battle was over, there lay around him the mounds of swords, spears and shields from a thousand soldiers. No such feat of battle had been performed before nor has it since.

Yet, it is a strange fact that, when modern men think of Samson, what they associate with him is the enchantress Delilah. They do not remember that he was a judge of the nation of Israel and a great warrior; they only remember him as the man who dissipated himself with adultery, a man who was beguiled by a woman, and the world has never forgotten this. Our world is not impressed by the accounts of Samson's superhuman strength, but they do remember his transgression.

WHY DO CHRISTIAN LEADERS SUCCUMB?

You may ask, "From your observation, why do Christian leaders commit adultery?" Immorality in the ministry is a complex issue involving a number of factors. Why do Christian leaders succumb? Why does anyone fall into the sin of immorality?

Usually, at the crux of the matter is the way the man or woman wiews himself. There can be low self-image; on the other hand, a person may feel himself to be invincible—powerful and all-important, incapable of being found out.

For example, among ministers, one rarely hears of a young preacher just beginning his ministry, striving to become successful, falling into adultery. It is usually the minister who is very successful and feels he has arrived at the top.

This same principle applies in the business world and the professional world. Very often it is the man or woman who has accomplished something in life; the ones who have achieved a measure of success. This abuse of power and position is a snare of the devil.

"Wherefore let him that thinketh he standeth take heed lest he fall" (1 Corinthians 10:12).

As long as David was fighting his battles, he was a true hero; but, when he had time to lounge upon his rooftop in idleness, he disgraced his name forever!

As long as Samson was destroying lions and fighting battles, he was the leader of his nation; but, when he took time to pursue his own pleasure, the devil deceived and destroyed him.

Friend, be careful of the moment in your life when you think you have achieved something and no longer need to struggle for success. Just then is when you are in an excellent position for the devil to damn your soul and cause you to sin!

Many reasons can enter in when one attempts to analyze why anyone becomes involved in moral failure. This book is not an attempt to do that. But, remember, we are not to be ignorant of Satan's devices. Be assured that God has said in His Word that "There hath no temptation taken you but such as is common to man: but God is faithful, who will not suffer you to be tempted above that you are able; but will with the temptation also make a way to escape, that ye may be able to bear it!" (1 Corinthians 10:13).

You must shun the evil of adultery as did Joseph (Genesis 39:1-12) when entreated by a desirable woman. Though his master's wife asked him to commit adultery with her, he ran away. She even grabbed his coat to hold him, but he left his coat and ran. She got the coat, but not Joseph's virtue. Because of his holiness and purity, Joseph is the most perfect type of Christ in the Old Testament. Now let us proceed to learn how to protect this hidden treasure of immortality.

4

PROTECTING THE IMMORTALITY OF MAN

> *Do not be unequally yoked together with unbelievers: for what fellowship has righteousness with lawlessness? And what communion has light with darkness? And what accord has Christ with Belial? Or what part has a believer with an unbeliever? And what agreement has the temple of God with idols? For you are the temple of the living God. As God has said: "I will dwell in them and walk among them. I will be their God, And they shall be My people."*
> 2 Corinthians 6:14-16 NKJ

> *But to the rest I, not the Lord, say: If any brother has a wife who does not believe, and she is willing to live with him, let him not divorce her.*
> *And a woman who has a husband who does not believe, if he is willing to live with her, let her not divorce him.*
> 1 Corinthians 7:12-13 NKJ

LET us consider one of the greatest sins against immortality in modern society.

First, we will look at God's reasoning in the matter.

From time immemorial, Jehovah-God commanded His people not to intermarry nor commit fornication with unbelievers and heathen. Many times in the Old Testament, God thus admonished His people. It is interesting to observe that when God would not permit the mysterious prophet named Balaam to curse the children of Israel, Balaam counseled with Israel's enemies (the Moabites and Midianites) to commit whoredom with Israel (see Numbers 31:15-16 and Numbers 25:3-5).

Because of that counsel, the sin of adultery became known as the doctrine of Balaam. In Revelation 2:14, Christ rebuked the church because she had gone into apostasy and said: ". . .I have a few things against thee, because thou hast there them that hold the doctrine of Balaam, who taught Balac to cast a stumblingblock before the children of Israel, to eat things sacrificed unto idols, and to commit fornication" (Revelation 2:14).

Why will God not permit a man or woman to marry whom he or she pleases? Why should there be restrictions? Why did the Word of God say: "Be ye not unequally yoked together with unbelievers. . ." (2 Corinthians 6:14).

It again brings us to the sacredness of that life which we can produce after our kind. God forbids Christians to form intimate relationships with unbelievers. The Bible refers to marriage as "being yoked together." God's Word commands that a Christian be not yoked with an incompatible (unbelieving) person. God further accentuated this when He said: ". . .what fellowship has righteousness with lawlessness? And what communion has light with darkness? And what accord has Christ with Belial? Or what what part has a believer with an unbeliever?" (2 Corinthians 6:14-15 NKJ).

God here is asking, "What do believers and unbelievers have in common?'' The Bible says the Christian is the temple of God (see 2 Corinthians 6:16). This being true, the opposite means that the sinner is the temple of Satan, the devil. How can these two become one, in producing posterity?

The Apostle Paul tells us in 1 Corinthians 12:27 that Christians are members of the body of Christ: ''Now you are the body of Christ, and members individually (NKJ).

How can you, therefore, as members of His body, be yoked with a person who is not of God?

This means that unequally yoked marriages are absolutely forbidden of God! Some of this modern generation say that love answers all questions but, when we read our daily newspapers and see that one out of every three marriages in America terminates in divorce, it is evident that love is not the answer to marital problems.

The prophet Amos, in chapter 3, verse 3, asks: ''How can two walk together, except they be agreed?''

God here is asking, ''How can a

young man and a young woman create
a happy home, unless both parties
have a personal faith in Christ." This
requires agreement in spiritual things,
expecially, as well as in all other
matters.

I have observed that, in many
divided homes, a man and woman
who are unequally yoked together
never see life the same. The Christian
will say, "I cannot do this and I cannot go there." Therefore, the result is
that the true Christian who marries an
unbeliever will live in continual con-
flict. The believer will say, "I want to
go to church," and the unbeliever will
say, "I do not want to go."

WHAT SHOULD BE DONE?

I have often been asked, "What
should we do when a man and woman
are already married and one of them
becomes a Christian?"

God's Word is careful to give us an
answer to this in 1 Corinthians 7:12-13.
". . .If any brother has a wife who does
not believe, and she is willing to live
with him, let him not divorce her.

"And a woman who has a husband who does not believe, if he is willing to live with her, let her not divorce him."

Therefore, you can see from the Word of God, the Christian is forbidden to leave the unbeliever. He or she must pray for them to be saved.

HOLY MATRIMONY

God has given the commands He has concerning this holy estate because the man and woman, who have been united in holy matrimony, will be creating immortal souls. With such a holy trust as marriage, God demands holiness and purity in His followers.

Today, divorce occurs three times as often in unequally yoked marriages as in marriages of the same faith.

An unequally yoked marriage is a mis-marriage. It destroys the divine nature of spiritual life. The two who create souls form one soul and spirit.

Dr. Billy Graham stated in his booklet, "The Answer to Broken Homes," that there is only one divorce to every

57 marriages where the families regularly attend church. He states further that statistics prove that there is only one divorce to every 500 marriages where there is regular daily prayer and Bible reading in the home!

MIS-MARRIAGE

The first unequally yoked marriage in Bible history, recorded in Genesis 6:2-5, tells of the sons of God being married to the daughters of men. This illegitimate relationship brought the anger of God upon the people of that generation, because their unions produced wild specimens of humanity. It produced terrible apostasy. It brought the great flood upon the human race.

MARRYING FOR SPITE

There are many reasons for mixed marriages.

Esau, a son of Isaac and the brother of Jacob, deliberately married a daughter of the land of Canaan, a heathen woman, to spite his parents (Genesis 28:8-9). His action brought a great division into the family of Israel, which remains unto this day. No doubt, many young people today marry for spite and, thereafter, live lives of eternal regret.

MARRYING FOR LUST

In Judges 14:2-3, 7, we read that Samson found a daughter of the Philistines who "pleased him well." This is an example of a man marrying for lust. He did not look for a godly girl, one who followed the law of God. This heathen girl pleased him.

To Samson's sorrow, however, he found that the heathen believed in divorce and remarriage and that they had taken his wife away from him and given her to another man. From this sin, Samson fell into the lowest wickedness, until he came under the power of the enchantress Delilah. No doubt, there are many youth today marrying for lust.

It always ends in spiritual ruin!

MARRYING FOR LUXURY

Marrying many princesses and strange women to engage in royal luxury caused King Solomon great sorrow. We read of this in I Kings 11:1-5. God chose Solomon to be king over His people Israel and enlarged his mental capacity to such an extent that he was known as the most brilliant and wisest man of all history. Yet, God's Word says that he desired and married the princesses of the neighboring kings. It was these sinful, heathen women who ultimately, when Solomon was old, turned his heart away from the Lord who had made him a great and wise king.

Nehemiah 13:26 says, "Did not Solomon king of Israel sin by these things? yet among many nations was there no king like him, who was beloved of his God, and God made him king over all Israel: nevertheless even him did outlandish women cause to sin."

MARRYING FOR ETERNITY

A Christian marriage will make a happy home. Christian homes will make a strong godly country. A Christian marriage means that both parties are Christian and they will have a family altar, where both pray together!

God has always wanted His righteous seed to be clean and pure.

When God chose the nation of Israel, he commanded them not to intermarry with other people. He demanded this because He knew that people produce after their kind, and that His people would soon be heathen if they married heathen. There is something very remarkable about who you marry. For example, in my family and also in my wife's family, there are many ministers. My mother could name twelve or fifteen ministers, most of them Methodist, of my uncles and great uncles. Two of my brothers are pastors, my sister is a minister, and counting through our two families there are about eighteen ministers. It is the same with my wife. Her people were Methodists. Her grandfather was a Methodist minister. Her mother was a minister. Her stepfather was a minister.

The records of our country show that not only does religion run in the bloodstream, but so does crime. The

F.B.I. has traced crime through families and found that it costs our country millions of dollars to pay for crime in certain families.

This means one should know what kind of family he or she is marrying into. We believe in the words, "holy matrimony" because it deals with the life force of the universe.

Millions of Americans think it does not matter whom they marry. Some feel they have a perfect right to yield to the lusts of their own desires and that is the reason the divorce courts are full of people! That is the reason the insane asylums are full. That is the reason there are so many children born sick and deformed.

When two people create a new life, these two people should be of the same spirit and of the same mind.

Do you believe that?

People who raise rabbits believe it!

People who raise hogs believe it!

Dairymen who raise fine cows believe it!

If right breeding is so important in animals, surely we can understand why God commanded us, as human beings created in His likeness, not to be unequally yoked together with unbelievers.

GOD AND DIVORCE

God forbids divorce because it prostitutes the sacred mystery of life. Divorce breaks the divine fellowship born in Eden the day God made Eve to live with Adam.

God ordained marriage to last as long as both persons live. On this question, Jesus said: ''The Pharisees also came to him, tempting him, and saying unto him, Is it lawful for a man to put away his wife for every cause?

''And he answered and said unto them, Have ye not read, that he which made them at the beginning made them male and female,

''And said, For this cause shall a man leave father and mother, and shall cleave to his wife: and they twain shall be one flesh?

''Wherefore they are no more twain, but one flesh. What therefore God hath joined together, let not man put asunder'' (Matthew 19:3-6).

It is remarkable that our Lord chose a marriage as the place to perform His first miracle. There were many hungry people, but He did not multiply bread first. There were many sick people, but He did not heal them first. He opened his miracle ministry by showing His love toward a newly married couple. Christ forever placed His sanction upon the same union that God created in Eden.

God makes no provision for divorce. When He created Adam and Eve, there was no greed, no selfishness, no hate, no misunderstanding, and no jealousies which cause divorce.

The Word of God in no place states that God has altered His divine principles in order to accommodate sinful men and women.

WHAT TO DO IF DIVORCED WHILE A SINNER

Many times I have been confronted by those who were divorced while yet in sin and were ignorant of God's law. They want to know if they should now separate even though, in many cases,

it would be impossible to be united
with their former companions who are
remarried and have children by other
companions. We believe that we are in
divine order when we say that when
you give your heart to Christ you must
start your new life from that moment.
Christ came not to destroy, He came
to fulfill. It would only create more
problems to break up your present
home. Therefore, we are sure that God
wants you to remain as you were
when you found Him.

AMERICA'S BROKEN HOMES

Some of the saddest people I meet
on the face of the earth are victims of
broken homes. The strength of our nation is the home. Our strength on the
battlefield, when our soldiers are
fighting for the existence of our nation, is the strength of the homes they
come from. When the home life of a
nation degenerates and disintegrates,
that nation is bound for oblivion.
Unless the American home can now
be strengthened in God, it will not
take Communism to destroy us; our

own disease of immorality will eat the vitals of our nation.

BROKEN HEARTS

One day I spoke to the boys in a juvenile detention home. One fine-looking young man said he was to be released soon. With great pride in his voice he said he had mowed lawns all over the area making money in order to change his name the day he left the reformatory. He said his parents had been in and out of jail so many times that even to bear their name would be a hindrance to his future. There are thousands of young people in our land who are brokenhearted today because of the broken homes they are a part of.

The hope of the home is not the divorce court. It is the sure word of God; it is the church that upholds the biblical standard.

It is time for the judge and the marriage counselor to turn to the Bible to find the answers for the multitudes of people seeking marital help. As God created male and female, so God only, can keep them together.

Millions of people today are afraid of their homes being broken. May I assure you that your only security for a happy home is in Christ Jesus. Place this motto on the wall of your home:

"Christ is the Head of this house,
The unseen Guest at every meal;
The silent Listener to every conversation."

Then have a family altar and worship together, read your Bible and pray together. By so doing, you will certainly have a happy Christian home!

THE DECEPTION OF SUICIDE

Let's go further with this truth of the mystery of life. Let's consider the matter of suicide—taking one's life. If a man or woman deliberately takes his or her life, he (or she) is tampering with the divine mystery of life, which is born of God and is unending.

This divine life within us is not ours to give or take.

Let it be clear that any man or woman in his or her right mind (we're not speaking of insane or irresponsible people), who conceives suicide and carries it out, whether by sleeping pills, violent poison or gun, is thwarting God's plan in that life. Every human must wait until God calls him to leave this stage of action. No man knows what tomorrow may bring.

In the Bible, which required Holy men inspired of God some 1,500 years to write, there are three outstanding suicides recorded. One was King Saul who was backslidden in spirit and defeated in battle (1 Samuel 31:4); the second was Ahithophel, David's counsellor. When he saw his cunning devices against David were not successful, he took his own life (2 Samuel 17:23). The third was Judas Iscariot. When he discovered that his thirty pieces of silver did not bring peace to his soul, he cast the money at the feet of the men who gave it to him and went out and hanged himself (Matthew 27:5).

These three men, one a king and warrior, one a philospher and thinker, and the third the treasurer for the group who followed Jesus (and one of His disciples), were all defeated men.

They had not relied upon God. The devil convinced each that to die by his own hand was the only way out.

Suicide is not the end. A person is only changing locations. We are immortal souls destined to live forever.

5

THE BATTLE FOR IMMORTALITY

Likewise as it was also in the days of Lot: They ate, they drank, they bought, they sold, they planted, they built;

but on the day that Lot went out of Sodom it rained fire and brimstone from heaven and destroyed them all.

Even so will it be in the day when the Son of Man is revealed.

Luke 17:28-30 NKJ

MANY thinking people of our generation are conscious that a cataclysmic event is imminent. They believe that there is sufficient evidence that we are nearing the end of time, as marked by man.

One of the sure signs of this approaching end of time is the moral degeneration of the human race. The Bible, in its prophetical books and passages, has predicted there would be a great moral decline among the human race at the end of time. Jesus said in Matthew 24:37; ". . .As the days of Noah were, so shall also the coming of the Son of man be" (NKJ).

In Genesis 6:1-7, we see what happened in Noah's day. It was wrong intermarriage which created a society of men so wicked that God repented that He had made them. The great sin which brought the flood was not commercial nor economic—it was moral sin.

Jesus predicted that, at the time of His second coming, the world would be in the same condition as it was in Noah and Lot's day (Luke 17:26-30).

There was a kingdom city named Sodom in Palestine. The Bible said that Sodom, at first, resembled the Garden of Eden because it was so beautiful. In this tropical paradise something strange happened. The men in that city decided they did not need women except to produce children; they decided that their sexual enjoyment would be with men. Their sin was so dreadful that for the past three thousand years the name of that city, which had once been so beautiful, has been associated with the sin of sodomy (homosexuality). God beheld this city of strange passions and saw how they were frustrating the divine purpose of God and the holy mystery of life, and God was angry. God's wrath was so intense that he sent fire out of the heavens and burned that city. As it sank into the ground, it became the bottom of the Dead Sea, which is the lowest spot on the face of the earth. It is over twelve hundred feet below sea level. Sodom, therefore, became the sore and remains the largest and ugliest scar on the face of the earth.

Why did God become so angry? Because the men of Sodom had left their normal functions, for which God had created them, and were using the divine purpose in the wrong way.

Lot was associated with a city which gave birth to the lowest moral standards in history. When man commits moral sin with another man, or a human being has sexual relations with an animal, the world calls it sodomy and beastiality.

This sin is probably becoming more widespread on the face of this earth today than any other. The natural impulses of men have been changed, perverted and twisted until he pollutes this mystery of life with the lowest human impulses, rather than being the creator with God to reproduce the human race.

In most countries, this sin is no longer looked down upon. Homosexuals are even trying to legitimize it. In all the large cities of the world, this sin has become a tremendous problem to the legal authorities.

When women commit this sin with women, it is called lesbianism. Almost any book store today displays books on the subject. Law authorities estimate that millions of men and women are involved in the homosexual and lesbian life-style.

The important thing I would again

call to your attention is that God destroyed the earth in Noah's day because of moral sin. Because of the prevalence of this moral sin in Sodom and Gomorrah, God became so indignant that He cursed and destroyed those cities. I repeat, their remains now lie at the bottom of the Dead Sea.

Much of the modern world today is shocked at the prevalence of this sin, but strong forces are conspiring to make homosexuality an acceptable and alternate life-style.

You may ask, "Brother Sumrall, if a person commits adultery, fornication or sodomy, can he be forgiven?"

Yes, he can. God will forgive every sin except the sin against the Holy Ghost, but personally I believe the most difficult sin for heaven to forgive is moral sin, because it deals with immortality—life that God created!

If every preacher in America would preach this message, if every high school teacher in America would present this truth to the youth of America, if every politician would advocate this truth, the smile and blessing of God would again come upon our land.

You can look into the faces of people on the streets today and see the price of sin stamped thereon. The lines of sin cannot be erased.

Friend, keep your soul clean! Keep your body clean morally!

How grateful I am for the thousands of God's people in our country who are living clean lives.

If you have already offended God in this matter, come to the old rugged cross and let the blood of Jesus cover your wretched life. Christ's blood will cover the sins of your life. It will blot into oblivion all your sin and you can live a holy life from this moment.

SEVEN PRECAUTIONS

Listed below are seven things you can do that will assure you a clean moral life:

1. Keep the right company; avoid evil companions, they will lead you astray.
2. Refuse to listen to immoral stories, whether on the radio or from the lips of companions.
3. Refuse to read pornographic

literature. We become what we read and put into our minds.

4. Refuse to look at obscene pictures, for such gives birth to moral degeneracy. (Numbers 33:52).

5. Never dress immorally. Your attire affects the morals of others and of yourself.

6. Never look upon a woman or a man to lust after her or him (Matthew 5:27-28).

7. Keep yourself pure. Never permit yourself to get into an embarrassing situation where the devil can take advantage of your good morals.

Because of the sin of immorality at the end of the age, inevitable judgment shall come upon the human race.

This divine judgment as a result of sin will come in the form of deformities in children and strange diseases in children and adults, such as AIDS.

Romans 1:18-27 speaks of the wrath of God coming upon all ungodliness and unrighteousness. The consequences of God's condemnation are divine abandonment: "Therefore God also gave them up to uncleanness, in the lusts of their hearts, to dishonor their bodies among themselves, who exchanged the truth of God for the lie, and worshipped and served the creature rather than the Creator who is blessed forever. Amen.

"For this reason God gave them up to vile passions. For even their women exchanged the natural use for what is against nature.

"Likewise also the men, leaving the natural use of the woman, burned in their lust for one another, men with men committing what is shameful, and receiving in themselves the penalty of their error which was due.

"And even as they did not like to retain God in their knowledge, God gave them over to a debased mind, to do those things which are not fitting; being filled with all unrighteousness, sexual immorality, wickedness. . ." (Romans 1:24-29a NKJ).

Deuteronomy 28:15-68 speaks of the disobedient children of Israel and the "plague" coming upon the people, "clinging to" and "destroying them" because of their wickedness. God carefully warns man in these passages, and in the New Testament passages such as Jude 1:7, and 1 Corinthians 10:1-11, citing sexual immorality as contributing to the downfall of these cities.

Finally, unless man repents, there will be an eternal hell for those who have tampered with the divine mystery of life.

God's warnings stand. He is not wanting any to perish. His love, forgiveness and restoration await all who will come to Him: "For God so loved the world that He gave His only begotten Son, that whoever believes in Him should not perish but have everlasting life.

"For God did not send His Son into the world to condemn the world, but that the world through Him might be saved.

"He who believes in Him is not condemned; but he who does not believe is condemned already, because he has not believed in the name of the only begotten Son of God" (John 3:16-18 NKJ).

YOU CAN KNOW GOD'S FORGIVENESS

You need a personal Savior, a personal commitment to Him who is able and willing to forgive you of ALL your sins. Pray this Sinner's Prayer, and really mean it. He will give you peace, joy, and hope!

"Lord Jesus, I am a sinner. I believe that you died and rose from the dead to save me from my sins. Father, forgive me for yielding the control of my mind to anyone other than You. Wash me with Your blood, and I shall be clean. I ask You into my heart right now. Be my Savior and my guide forever. Amen."

In your flesh, you may not FEEL any different. But, the Word of God tells us that you are now a New Creature, and old things are passed away and forgiven. You are no longer under condemnation. You are in Christ Jesus and you now walk after the Spirit (Romans 8:1, II Corinthians 5:17, I John 2:12, Luke 7:47).

Now that you have become a child of God, please write us and we'll send you some literature to help you walk daily with the Lord. Write to: **LeSEA,** P.O. Box 12, South Bend, IN 46624. **24-hour Prayerline: (219) 291-1010.**

GLOBAL
FEED-THE-HUNGRY PROGRAM

You are invited to join LeSEA's End-Time Joseph Program to help feed Christians who live in areas plagued by famine. While he was in Israel with a group of pilgrims, the Lord asked Dr. Sumrall to initiate a global program to combat hunger and he was told in detail how to tackle such a herculean task. God declared that the aggressive attack against the forces of evil should be three-pronged. How can this be done?

Seminars will be held in famine stricken areas when the people are ministered to spiritually. We will pray for the sick and deliver those in bondage. Pastors will then be given food and other supplies which they will distribute among their own congregations. This will elevate the pastor in the eyes of their people.

We are looking for 10,000 pastors to challenge world hunger by including "Feed the Hungry" in their missionary giving. For more information, write:

**FEED THE HUNGRY, South Bend, IN
46680-7777 USA**

Let us hear from you today. We must act now! Tomorrow may be too late!